What people are saying about

Since We Saw Yo- ----

Having experienced Ben _____ 'ogether
in a parish setting, I knov _____ ...most a pastor
with a deep passion for ___ every God-given moment to
celebrate with our community', meeting the needs of ordinary
people 'as and when they touch-base with us' – especially in
those liminal moments of birth and marriage, life and death. I
also know that he has a gift for crafting group (and individual)
Bible Studies that actually work! I can heartily recommend
this series of studies, making vivid and thought-provoking
connections between Gospel and culture, and taking us into a
deeper understanding both of our shared humanity and of the
God who comes to us and loves us where we are.
Canon Professor Loveday Alexander, Canon Theologian
Emeritus, Chester Cathedral

This book is a great resource for small groups. Ben helps us
explore a range of life's rites of passage by reflecting afresh
on the 'I am' sayings of Jesus. He draws on the music of Gary
Barlow, adds in well-chosen references to an eclectic range of
films and TV programmes, and skilfully combines this all with
scripture and other Christian resources. The result is engaging,
thought-provoking and inspiring. It will challenge Christians to
think again about how to build positive relationships with those
around them; it will challenge those who are not yet Christian
to recognise the Good News that Jesus offers. This is a great
resource for churches looking to grow as faithful and vibrant
communities of faith.
Rev Leslie Newton, Chair, Yorkshire North and East Methodist
District

Ben provides us with a series of Bible studies which relates scripture to living in the twenty-first century. The illustrations he uses are current and bring meaning and understanding to the scripture being studied. The word games and devices that he has developed to help us wrestle with the text are relevant and will enable disciples today to grow in faith and to once again fall in love with reading and studying the Bible. I cannot recommend these studies too highly; they are Bible studies you will utilise time and time again for personal study, the leading of worship, as well as with groups. A must buy.

Rev Loraine Mellor, President of British Methodist Church 2017/18

It's encouraging to know that one of the biggest trends across the worldwide church today is a re-discovering of our need to disciple people. After all, that is the call of every follower of Jesus – to be a disciple and make more! Ben's passion for the church and hunger to see people connect with God, in a real and authentic way, is evident throughout these studies. He's woven together contemporary illustration with scriptural foundations that will help anyone who undertakes them to discover a fresh depth and insight with regards to the Bible, but also help to take their next steps in their own personal walk with Jesus.

Pastor Chris Denham, Lead Pastor, Hope City Church, Leeds

Since We Saw You Last
You Last

The Church, The Community and
Rites of Passage

Since We Saw You Last

The Church, The Community and Rites of Passage

Ben Clowes

CIRCLE
BOOKS

Winchester, UK
Washington, USA

JOHN HUNT PUBLISHING

First published by Circle Books, 2019
Circle Books is an imprint of John Hunt Publishing Ltd., No. 3 East St., Alresford,
Hampshire SO24 9EE, UK
office@jhpbooks.com
www.johnhuntpublishing.com
www.circle-books.com

For distributor details and how to order please visit the 'Ordering' section on our website.

Text copyright: Ben Clowes 2018

ISBN: 978 1 78904 327 3
978 1 78904 328 0 (ebook)
Library of Congress Control Number: 2019933925

A CIP catalogue record for this book is available from the British Library.

Design: Stuart Davies

UK: Printed and bound by CPI Group (UK) Ltd, Croydon, CR0 4YY
US: Printed and bound by Thomson Shore, 7300 West Joy Road, Dexter, MI 48130

We operate a distinctive and ethical publishing philosophy in
all areas of our business, from our global network of authors to
production and worldwide distribution.

Contents

To my wonderful wife, whose taste in music led to these studies.

To me, rites of passage through life, that's a wonderful, beautiful thing.
Lance Henriksen

Foreword

I am deeply indebted to the Methodist Church of Great Britain for their clear policy of giving their ministers times of Sabbatical. In the weeks and months preceding mine in 2016 I was looking forward to a break from the normal routine and whilst I had intended to write a Bible study, this wasn't the one I had in mind! I need to thank my former and present church contexts for allowing me to trial these on them. Many people encouraged me to seek publication but I particular need to note Ruth James and Denise Archer for their constant pushing. I should also note former and current colleagues in both the Methodist and Anglican churches who have found these studies useful in their contexts.

I also need to thank my family – my mum and dad for their commitment to show me their own personal faith in action and for my wonderful wife, Catherine, and my boys, Sam and Joel for their ability to listen to my ramblings and still find ways to sound so utterly supportive.

Ultimately, I need to thank God for his gifts and for the way my Sabbatical was used not only to deepen my own faith but to discover more of his calling on my life.

I trust that you will find these studies as useful in your churches and in your own personal life as I have had in putting them together.

Acknowledgements

New International Version (NIV)

Holy Bible, New International Version® Anglicized, NIV® Copyright © 1979, 1984, 2011 by Biblica, Inc.® Used by permission. All rights reserved worldwide.

These Scriptures are copyrighted and have been made available on the Internet for your personal use only. Any other use including, but not limited to, copying or reposting on the Internet is prohibited. These Scriptures may not be altered or modified in any form and must remain in their original context. These Scriptures may not be sold or otherwise offered for sale.

These Scriptures are not shareware and may not be duplicated.

These Scriptures are not public domain.

New Revised Standard Version (NRSV)

Some scripture quotations are from New Revised Standard Version Bible: Anglicized Edition, copyright © 1989, 1995 National Council of the Churches of Christ in the United States of America. Used by permission. All rights reserved worldwide.

New Living Translation (NLT)

Scripture quotations marked (NLT) are taken from the Holy Bible, New Living Translation, copyright ©1996, 2004, 2015 by Tyndale House Foundation. Used by permission of Tyndale House Publishers, Inc., Carol Stream, Illinois 60188. All rights reserved.

Introduction & How to Use These Studies

In the twenty-first century it would appear, with the stories of decline in membership and attendance at churches in the Western World, that society has finished with church. If this is the case and society no longer has any need of our services, why does the church have so many problems closing or modernising our ancient and often under-used buildings? There are so many stories of churches which have an average attendance in single figures who have come to the difficult decision that the faith journey of that Christian community is complete only to have people who have never been seen for years to turn out to complain! This is a great challenge for those seeking to move Christian communities forward, particularly those who have become fairly stuck in their ways.

The church that we are talking about here is the community of people who are meeting in Jesus' name week in, week out but we do need to remember that society often sees the church as the edifice, the building, that will always be there when they need it but won't interfere in their lives in between. The local society likes to be able to use 'their' church for their celebrations – for the oft quoted 'hatching, matching and despatching' (births, marriages and funerals).These people rarely, if ever, give any thought to the church members who keep the place in a good condition, pay all the bills and faithfully worship week in, week out. As a church leader, I can think of many people who I have seen in church only very occasionally but call those particular buildings 'their' church. Extrapolating that could mean that most local folk turn up about ten times in their whole lives and this is decreasing with the increasing usage of secular 'celebrants', particularly for funerals! What does the church have to say to these people and to the church in these situations? What do we need to do to find out what has happened since we last saw them?

There are those church members who would have the church solely for the use of those who regularly put their money in the pot as they are the ones who work hard and are committed to the work of God. There are also those who can see the importance of 'being there' for the community. This leaves us with the problem of how we build better links with those 'using' the church but, with declining congregations, it is the something we need to work out. Ultimately, we need to answer the question of how we engage with the community we only see very irregularly, having conversations with them when we do see them, sharing God's good news with them – even if we're not totally aware of the things that have happened in their lives since we saw them last.

I actually believe the church has a lot to learn here. Our focus is too often on 'bums on seats', we spend our lives counting people in and out in many denominations, sometimes, I believe, to the detriment of actually meeting the needs of the community as and when they touch-base with us. The counting serves a purpose of reporting Christianity's general decline in the Western World but the faith is blossoming in places and situations where we get the priorities in the right order! Of course, in the twenty-first-century post-modern climate we have had to seek new and innovative ways of increasing the potential for moments when church and community meet, but I also believe that we're not always the best at taking every God-given moment to celebrate with our community. John Wesley spoke of the means of grace and converting ordinances. He recognised that in the Book of Acts, God used a multiplicity of ways (means of grace) of sharing his love, not just 'churchy' things.[1] He also noted that during his life he had encountered many for whom church events, such as Holy Communion, had been a time of conversion (converting ordinances) and of meeting with the prevenient grace of God himself.[2] These are the times, liminal moments, when we should be seizing the opportunity to share the gospel, not in a 'I'm going to force this down your throat' way but by trying to find new approaches which sow seeds. Some of this will naturally come from the fact that we too face the same life-moments, the same dilemmas, the same crises. Being Christian doesn't make us immune to this. We need to also remember that Jesus too faced much of the same issues as 'the Word made flesh'. It is, for me, one of the greatest wonders of the Christian faith that God would choose to 'empty himself of all but love'[3] and be clothed in human form. I believe we need to hear Jesus saying to each of those who 'use' our churches 'how have you been since I saw you last?'.

As Christians we talk of having a personal relationship with Jesus but I wonder how many of us actively work at this? How many of us are more bothered with the general administration of our church edifices rather than worshipping the God they were built to worship? Do we know Jesus personally in our everyday lives – because how can we expect to share him with others if we have no personal knowledge and understanding of the 'God with skin on'? When we come to those crisis moments, are we too meeting with Jesus for the first time in a long while? Does he also say to us – how have you been since I saw you last?

Much of this occurs because there is a danger that Jesus becomes another character in a story, a 'name' like a fictional character but one who we have come to know only through the words we have read but not engaged with in our hearts. These studies were originally designed for a group but are equally suitable for individuals to use as personal study. They work through the different 'I am' sayings of Jesus in John's gospel, claims of who he is which challenged the perceptions of those he knew in first-century Palestine, but are equally challenging for us today. They are symbolic of first-century thinking and imagery but I am not sure Jesus would change the imagery much for our twenty-first-century Western eyes. Maybe we need a little assistance to engage with this – and this is where Gary

Barlow's music comes in!

Life is full of emotions and *Since I saw you last* – Gary Barlow's 2013 solo album is full of them. The story of the difficult path that Gary's life had taken – after the break-up of Take That in the 1990s, his vilification by the press, his re-found success during the 2000s and the difficulties in his life such as the stillbirth of his daughter Poppy – are echoed in the emotions of the lyrics of every song on the album. They link with six natural 'rites' of passage, times when our communities reach out to the church – birth, adolescence, marriage, searching for meaning, times of crisis and endings of life. There are two songs on the album for each of these times each matching with one of the 'I am' sayings of Jesus in John's Gospel. As I have shared these studies, people have been intrigued with some of his lyrics on this album, particularly in the song 'God'. Gary has been quoted as saying that 'I do pray, I pray a lot … I don't know if there's a God but I do say prayers, and I say prayers for people. There are no answers on this record but there are considerations and questions of the whole idea around it'.[4] There certainly is a lot of searching on the album and I believe it is this which can open the door to our searching too.

Through these studies it is my hope that Christians will find new ways to connect with their communities, to be touched themselves in their liminal moments with God and learn to be a place of transition and meeting for those who 'use' our buildings, so that we all might hear God saying, 'how have things been since we saw you last?'.

How to use these studies

These studies are written so that they can be easily used by groups or individuals. They follow a standardised and well-tried fourfold format of 'Welcome', 'Worship', Word' and 'Witness'. Each session is timed to last 90 minutes and there are indications at the beginning of each section to keep you to time.

Welcome – encourages people to be open and part of the group with what might seem frivolous sometimes, but the questions are linked to the subject matter in some way. In each case I will offer some ideas but do use your own – you know your group better than I do! If you are using these studies for yourself it is still important to use this section to prepare yourself to study God's word.

Worship – the early church worshipped together in homes, and so should the twenty-first-century church and there are lots of different ways of doing this. In each session the main text includes a basic worship structure, but there are other resources listed in the Worship Materials chapter. However you structure the worship, you are encouraged to use a verse of the hymn *Lord of all Hopefulness*, the words of which link so well with the themes of these studies and are freely available in many hymn books and online. The original hymn has only 4 verses so I have written two new verses to match sessions 2 and 5 which I hope you will find helpful; these are also listed in the Worship Materials chapter. You will need to have copies of the lyrics available for the worship time plus either some live music, if you are lucky enough to have a piano and piano player, or a CD/digital copy. There are several good instrumental versions on YouTube which could be streamed.

Word – the reason for the sessions is ultimately to study the Word of God in a deeper way. This section should take the longest.

Witness – this section tries to answer the 'so what' question, as I believe that meeting with God in Scripture should leave us changed and make us better witnesses for him.

Throughout the text of the sessions, each line begins with a keyword which indicates, if you are using these in a group context, the suggested way that the text is used:

'Link' – is designed as input for a leader to give.

'Neighbour' – is intended to encourage one-to-one sharing,

as this encourages the quieter ones to engage. This is sometimes followed by a plenary space for feedback from some of the group but some 'neighbour' questions deliberately have no feedback for the wider group so people may have more confidence to speak if they know they will not have to share. If 'no plenary' is noted, ensure the group know this is the case before setting them off in pairs.

'Question' – is designed as a group-wide discussion question.

If you are leading a group, all the notes will be in line with the text.

If you are using these studies as an individual, pause on each question and think through your answer and use the 'neighbour' parts to reflect deeper, maybe even finding space to share your thinking with someone else, even encouraging them to work through the material separately but at the same time and then, maybe, meeting up to chat.

The Background Material chapter contains some thoughts on John's Gospel and the 'I am' sayings which feed into all the studies and can act as background to any discussions. These thoughts are not offered as a theological treatise but, with my background as a pastoral theologian, as insights gained from my own reading of commentaries and other theological books, none of which can substitute one's own research, reading and reflection.

I always ask different group members to read the Bible readings as it encourages them to engage with the passages from lots of different versions and often opens up different insights.

On a practical note, each of these studies uses tracks from *Since I saw you last* by Gary Barlow. You will need a copy of the CD or the tracks which can be easily found on official music download sites. Some groups may find it helpful to see copies of the lyrics and these can be easily found on the web.

Background Material

Working with the dying is like being a midwife for this great rite of passage of death. Just as a midwife helps a being take their first breath, you help a being take their last breath.
Ram Dass[1]

Over many years of ministry so many people have talked to me, particularly on funeral visits, about how death is the one inevitability of life. We live life today in much the same way as our forebears – we are born, we live, we love, we have life problems, we die. Life goes on – an ever-flowing stream. It could seem as if life is an utterly futile existence where we are simply walking a treadmill to death, without any actual progression! But this can't be the 'life in all its fullness'[2] that Christ promised to give us, surely! Surely there is more to life than the endless days. Surely there is more to life 'under the sun', unless the writer of Ecclesiastes is right that it is all 'vanity of vanities'[3] and 'a chasing after the wind'.[4]

It is a human trait to mark the different things that make us human, things that mark our place on this mortal coil! At the heart of the Christian faith is the story of the incarnate God, the Word made flesh. As Paul puts in his letter to the Philippian church that Jesus:

> who, though he was God, he did not think of equality with God as something to cling to. Instead, he gave up his divine privileges; he took the humble position of a slave and was born as a human being.[5]

If life was so pointless then why would God create it and why would he send Jesus to live it? From the gospel stories we know that in Jesus' own life on earth, he was born, he went through childhood and teenage years (and all that that would have brought with it!), he had friends and suffered the emotion of watching them die, he even suffered crises in his own life such as the state he found himself in as he prayed in the Garden of Gethsemane. We have a 'God with skin on' who through Jesus knows what it is like to live the life we live and even to go through the death we all face and yet the great paradox is that Jesus, although human, was still God. John even begins his gospel account reminding us of this fact: 'In the beginning was the Word, and the Word was with God, and the Word was God.'[6]

So, if we see the humanity of Jesus in the things he encountered and did, how do we see the divinity of Jesus? Each of the gospels shows this in several ways, particularly through his teaching and miracle-laden ministry but John goes the extra step as he uses two words that would, in first-century Palestine, have been tantamount to a claim to divinity which in the Greek New Testament is written as εγο ειμι (ego eimi) meaning 'I am'! Words that could be used in the same way that we might use them today to declare 'I am English' or 'I am a Christian' or even 'I am what I am'! But here is the link, the Hebrew version of εγο ειμι takes us into Exodus 3:14 where Moses is meeting with God at the Burning Bush and trying to find out from God who he should say has sent him to Pharaoh.

> God said to Moses, 'I AM WHO I AM. This is what you are to say to the Israelites: I AM has sent me to you.'[7]

The phrase in Hebrew translated as 'I am', often written as YHWH, is still seen today as an unpronounceable name for God. In Jewish tradition, knowing someone's name meant you knew all about them, so God gives an unpronounceable name, one which is too holy to be used, as no human could ever know everything about Him! You can imagine the uproar among the religious classes as Jesus went around Israel declaring 'I am'!

This was a human claiming to be God. In John 10:33, Jesus is about to be stoned by the religious leaders because '... you, a mere man, claim to be God'.[8]

So, what are the 'I am' sayings? When you meet someone new you often try to assess what they are like and that is exactly what people at the time of Jesus were doing. From the disciples – 'Who is this? Even the wind and the waves obey him'[9] and the city of Jerusalem 'When Jesus entered Jerusalem, the whole city was stirred and asked "Who is this?"'[10] to the religious leaders '"Who are you?" they asked. "Just what I have been claiming all along," Jesus replied,'[11] everyone was seeking an answer to the question 'who is this man?'. Jesus continues to slowly reveal himself, through his teaching, his miracles and, in John's gospel, through the 'I am' sayings. Traditionally, there are seven 'I am' sayings – the bread of life, the light of the world, the gate, the good shepherd, the resurrection and the life, the way, the truth and the life, and the vine. But actually, there are at least 45 occurrences in John's gospel alone which are translated into English 'I am' and 25 of those are from the emphatic form of the verb using εγο ειμι. An obvious addition to the 'traditional seven' is found in Jesus' encounter with the Samaritan woman at the well when the woman has spoken of her faith in the coming Messiah, Jesus responds 'I am he, the one who is speaking to you'.[12]

Through these sayings Jesus not only draws attention to himself but also continues to reveal more of who God is. In the Old Testament we are told of a God who provides (Jehovah Jireh – Genesis 22:14), a God who is our banner (Jehovah Nissi – Exodus 17:15), a God who is our peace (Jehovah Shalom – Judges 6:24), a God of strength (Elohai Mauzi – Psalm 43:2), a God who is near (Elohai Mikarov – Jeremiah 23:23) and so the list goes on. The 'I am' sayings are part of this tradition. No one knows the name of God but through these statements we know some of his attributes and how is he is interested in every part of our lives.

For Christians this is one of the greatest comforts; we believe in a God who knows us, knows what it is to live, knows the direction we are taking and is also our provider, our banner, our peace, our strength and is near to us no matter what. What a wonderful God we serve!

All this is very well for Christians to believe in but how does this affect the world around us? In the twenty-first-century Western World we are witnessing a continued decline in church attendance, particularly in the more traditional denominations, and an increase in the secularisation of our society. People no longer necessarily know the stories of the Christian faith as the standard RE teaching in schools has been overtaken by a need to explore the plurality of faiths in society. Churches can no longer assume the traditional stories and aspects of church life many Christians were taught in Sunday Schools for centuries, are as ingrained in people's psyche. Try asking most school groups (and even many groups of adults) to pray the Lord's Prayer out loud and many will struggle! If you were to ask them to quote an 'I am' saying, most would fail. I have even had people look utterly vague when I have mentioned the stories like Noah! Yet, the imagery is still vibrant and, although many in our pluralistic society would resist some of the imagery and even the claims that Jesus makes, they offer so much to a society that is crying out for a friend who knows what it's like to be 'me'. We have a God who knows what it's like to be each and every one of us and still wants to be our friend!

Many in our world today are searching for a way to give life meaning and purpose; the church tries to help by offering points of contact (rites of passage), ways to mark the incessant inevitability of life. From moments of beginning and great joy (baptism), through times of learning and commitment (confirmation), love (marriage), life difficulties (confession), steps of faith (Christian renewal) and even death (funeral), there is something for every stage of life as the world seeks to find ways to express itself. Many express their searching through their taste in music. Researchers at North Carolina State University did some research in 2014 that looked at what the top ten themes in the lyrics of songs were in the US Top 100 between January 1960 and December 2009; their results showed these ten themes to be loss, desire, aspiration, nostalgia, pain, breakup, rebellion, inspiration, jadedness, escapism, desperation, confusion.[13] Each of these are part of the human condition, part of being who we are. If these themes are part of being human, they are also part of being church and, through the Word made flesh, part of God's understanding of us.

It was as I began to explore this concept to fashion these study sessions reflecting on the links between the 'I am' sayings and the stages of life that the church celebrates, that a fortuitous event happened. As I headed to a retreat house to do the work, I realised that the only CD left in the car was Gary Barlow's 2013 album *Since I saw you last*. I must thank my wife for this! As I was reflecting on the theme of church celebrations (e.g., baptisms, weddings, funerals), I realised our opening words with those we have seen before but only at a previous 'celebration', are often something on the lines of how things have been 'since we saw you last'! Church for many has become a centre for celebrating 'hatches, matches and dispatches' and very little else. Gary even quotes this famous phrase in the opening words of the first song on this album, 'Requiem'. I then noticed each song on the album makes some interesting observations that speak into this subject. In 'Let me go' (which Gary has said was written from the point of view of his stillborn baby girl, Poppy), he speaks of sadness, a broken heart and the search for understanding why things happen, but there's a sense of hopelessness in the words that nothing can make this better. In 'This House' he notes that our homes are often places of discord and harmony where life in all its fullness is displayed. As I listened to the album it was the song

'God' that struck me to indicate the heart of Gary's searching. The challenge to the church to share God struck me as strongly as the words of Jesus in the Great Commission:

> Therefore go and make disciples of all nations, baptising them in the name of the Father and of the Son and of the Holy Spirit, and teaching them to obey everything I have commanded you. And surely, I am with you always, to the very end of the age.[14]

Many of the words in the songs on the album are ones which we hear people outside the church speaking as they search for meaning in life, maybe not in such wonderfully lyrical ways as those Gary uses in his song-writing.

So, if people are searching for meaning in their lives, we need to speak into this as Christians and I believe this is at the heart of the links between the 'I am' sayings, rites of passage and the words we hear so eloquently put by Gary Barlow. We need to be a people who reach out and share the good news of Jesus' love with the world. We also need to remember that just as we are asking people how they have been 'since we saw them last' as they attend the 'irregular' celebrations of baptisms, weddings, funerals etc., they are asking if anything has changed which might enable them to take a step of faith, since they saw us last! These are also moments of opportunity for us to reflect how God meets with us, as we are people seeking words that help in our survival, direction, security, eternity, peace and purpose too.

These six studies, using the songs of Gary Barlow, the rhythm of the church's liturgy and the 'I am' sayings (and note they use the 'Gate' and 'Shepherd' passage as one entity here), are designed to help us work out our answers for those beyond the church as they come to us for words which will help in their life journey. What will you say to them as they come to

14

you and ask 'what new thing can you tell me about God in this new situation I am in?'. Maybe our answer needs to be 'let me tell you about the God who has been working in my life, *since we saw you last*'!

Session 1 – Birth and Childhood

Background information

It's often said by people outside the church that its main purpose is being there for 'hatches, matches and dispatches' (i.e. baptisms, weddings and funerals) and it doesn't matter what happens in the church in between and also what we believe (as long as it isn't pushed down throats) as long as the church can perform its duty in the rites of passage we all face. In so many ways this is a poor state of affairs and a sign of the consumerist society in the twenty-first-century Western World. There is a general malaise of wanting to 'consume' the church's celebrations at key moments of our lives but having no care of how it is funded and maintained in between times and there is certainly a lack of being bothered by what it believes. The church sees this from a very different point of view. These steps on the journey of life can be seen as opportunities to share the Gospel message but I wonder how often the opportunity is taken. This study looks at the opportunities offered through birth and childhood. One of the biggest opportunities in this time that the church has is in the Christian celebration of baptism, when people come to use the church to get their baby 'christened'. Whilst not all Christian traditions celebrate infant baptism, it is important to think about the ways the church interacts with babies and children, whether this is through full infant baptism, a thanksgiving service or even just a Christening (or naming) ceremony. It is also important to focus on the work the church can and does do with pre-teens.

Preparations

For each of these studies you will need to make decisions in advance on how you structure the worship time i.e. either using the worship suggested in the session or using another worship liturgy as suggested in the Worship Materials chapter. If your group would find it helpful to read the words to the Gary Barlow tracks used in the study, you will need to access these from one of the many online sources. You will need a way of playing the two tracks needed during the session and the music/lyrics to 'Lord of all Hopefulness'.

Welcome (10 mins)

Question: What was your favourite food as a child and why?

Neighbour: Share with your neighbour your earliest memory and also whether you had a good childhood (no plenary).

Link: So, let's head back to the beginning! When we think about most people's connection with church in the twenty-first-century Western World, we can probably guess the main points of contact will be at 'hatching, matching and dispatching' ceremonies (baptisms, weddings, funerals). We may even note the opportunities at other points on the journey of life where there are moments of faith, loss, crisis and even joy. Most Christian traditions have some form of celebration offered to parents and families at the birth of a child (e.g., Baptism, Thanksgiving, Christening) and there is a lot of evidence that churches who invest in workers with children and families are often churches that are growing. The oft-quoted adaptation of the African proverb about a village is true – it does take a whole church to raise a child.[1]

Question: What does your church offer to families with newborns and children up to pre-teens and what part do you play in this work?

Link: These studies are designed to make us think about ways in which we are connecting with families outside the church and also things we could do better. Each step of our life makes us into the people we are and as church we need to be involved in this. Our experiences can be reflected in the ways we speak, act and even just appear. It can be reflected in our work, our leisure and the way we bring up our families. These studies also link with the 2013 album by Gary Barlow, *Since I saw you last*, which for many critics is seen as a work reflecting the experience he had in his vilification by the media after the initial breakup of Take That in the 1990s, his subsequent re-found fame when they reformed in the 2000s and his other life experiences such as the death of his Father and the circumstance of his stillborn daughter Poppy. Many of these experiences can be heard in his lyrics as a voice of those who connect with the church in the 'hatching, matching and dispatching' moments.

Worship (10 mins)

Link: Each session focuses on a different season of life and is split into four sections – 'Welcome', 'Worship', 'Word' and 'Witness'. We begin with an introductory welcome to get us thinking about the subject followed by a time of worship. This leads into some time reflecting on God's Word and what Jesus had to say in these situations using the 'I am' sayings in John's Gospel, ending with the question of what difference this makes as we witness in the twenty-first century. There are links to the different liturgies and services for different seasons of life. At this point it is worth noting that we often relate different parts of life to times of the day and this is reflected in the choices of elements for our times of worship together. For the word and witness sections, we will remember the different liturgies of the church but for our worship we will link to their input at different times of day. We will use a verse of the same hymn each session (extended specifically for these studies). As we are thinking in this session about birth and baptism, our worship is focused on the dawn of the day.

Worship: Choose either the worship structure listed below or use a relevant resource for the beginning of the day, some options are listed in the Worship Materials chapter. Use verse 1 of Lord of all Hopefulness which speaks of the break or dawn of the day.

Pray: Opening Prayer.

Read: Psalm 95:1–7.

Pray: Prayer giving thanks for the morning.

Read or sing: Lord of all Hopefulness v1.

Pray: Lord's Prayer.

Pray: Closing Prayer leading into the session.

Word (40 mins)

Question: We begin this part of each session with 'Word play' – using word association. What is the first word that comes into your mind when you hear the following words: child, toddler, baby, birth. What other words for those early years of life would you use?

Neighbour: For those parents present, describe the first moment you saw your first baby? For those who aren't parents talk about being an auntie or uncle or a friend's baby you have had contact with. Please note it is okay if it wasn't a positive experience (no plenary)!

Link: Our lives are full of experiences, lots of ups and downs and we bring all of those to these studies. Some will have found the last question difficult to answer, it will have brought difficult times or feelings to mind. For others it will have been one of the most special moments they have ever had. These studies are an opportunity to reflect on the experiences we have faced in our lives and that others face in theirs and they are intended to provide space for us to think through the ups and downs of life and in doing so to see how, as Christians, the Gospel message can speak into others' lives too. Many of the key moments of our lives are marked by the church in rites of passage, moments of liturgy, times of 'contact'. These are opportunities for the church to share the good news but do we know what we should be saying? Do we know how people are feeling? Do people truly share what they are thinking?

Neighbour: How comfortable are you in sharing your faith

with family and friends? With strangers?

Plenary.

Link: In 2013, Gary Barlow released the album *Since I saw you last*. In the lyrics Gary seems to speak into many of the situations of life from a position of experience, of love, of loss, of birth and death. With the success that Gary now has it might seem to be an odd person to have as a backdrop to these studies but this album speaks directly out of the life experiences that Gary has lived in the spotlight of the media.

Neighbour: Share a positive and a negative experience of life which makes you the person you are (no plenary).

Link: These studies do not necessarily use Gary's tracks in the same sentiment as if he were here singing them but, looking at the lyrics and thinking of the theme should spark some thoughts.

Question: What sort of phrases from the Bible come to mind when we think about what Jesus had to say about 'life' (we're asking here about Bible verses which speak into different aspect of life)?

Link: What Jesus shared with us is life itself. A lot of what the church has to say comes from the fact that Jesus is God-incarnate. John 1:14 reminds us that Jesus is 'the Word made flesh'. He is fully human, i.e. he was born, felt emotion and died a painful death, yet he is also fully divine. One of the ways that John marks this in his gospel is through the 'I am' sayings. It is this connection which we will be exploring. So, in our exploration of life events we begin with the beginning – birth and the first of Gary Barlow's tracks which is actually the last one on the album!

Play: Track 12 'More than Life'.

Neighbour: Thinking about the lyrics of the song and the theme of 'birth and childhood' what are your reflections?

Plenary.

Question: What do babies actually do?

Question: What do babies need?

Link: When we're considering babies, it is all about survival and that's the theme of the first 'I am' saying.

Read: John 6:25–51.

Question: What is the context of this passage? (It follows the feeding of the 5000.)

Question: In v25–26, what do the people actually want? (They think they want bread but Jesus wants to give them something else!)

Link: There is a link here to v30 where Jesus speaks about the manna the Israelites had in the desert during the Exodus.

Question: Why do they ask what they must do in v28? (This is about people searching for God and trying to understand the rules they needed to follow to have life.)

Question: What do you know about first-century bread?

Link: At Passover bread was unleavened but it was always freshly-baked except on Sabbath when baked the previous day. Everyone always had bread in the house in case of visitors.

Question: Who has eaten bread today?

Link: At one time, bread was a staple in the UK but now our diet is much more varied and includes a lot of pasta and rice among other things. Bread really was a staple food for the poorer folk in first-century Palestine. It was sometimes all they could get to eat. It was a food for survival. It provided the nutrients for growth and health; it kept people sufficed.

Question: What is our spiritual bread? (Think here about the ways we can gain the nutrients for spiritual growth and health we need.)

Question: What is the difference between manna and Jesus' bread?

Link: The people are seeking a miracle so they can say Jesus is a prophet as Moses was. Jesus came to meet our needs in a different way. It is worth noting the many links here to Holy Communion.

Neighbour: Do you look for poor quality spiritual bread that just keeps you from hunger rather than the spiritual artisan loaf that Jesus is offering?

Read: Philippians 4:4,11–13.

Question: What does Paul have to say to us on this subject? (Paul is speaking of our need to be content in Christ.)

Witness (15 mins)

Link: In the service of 'Baptism for those of Riper Years' in the Book of Common Prayer, the text says 'Grant that all carnal affections may die in them, and that all things belonging to the Spirit may live and grow in them'.[2] In our churches in the twenty-first century we are continually seeking ways to reach out to younger generations through Family Workers, baptisms and schools work.

Question: What does your church offer to bury the 'carnal affections' of all humans?

Question: How is the spiritual bread your church offers perceived?

Question: What do non-Christians think about church?

Neighbour: When was the last time you offered Jesus to someone as their spiritual daily bread (no plenary)?

Link: The second Gary Barlow track today, to give us food for thought, is one Gary wrote about the concept of 'home'; I wonder if the same words could be seen as applicable to church?

Play: Track 10 'This House'.

Worship: Space to reflect in silence.

Pray.

Session 2 – Choices and Learning

Background notes

Having teenage children myself, as I write these studies, I think it's safe to say that I've learnt that it is impossible to be an expert on these years of human life! These are the years in which we begin to make lots of choices about our lives – from the subjects we want to study further at school, college and university to the friends we make and, in some cases, those people we wish to spend our lives with. There is the pain of physical growth, the changes in the hormones and falling in and out of love and friendships to contend with. All this with a backdrop of heading towards the peak of brain capacity around the age of 18. It is a time of choices and often learning from those choices the hard way! This time of life is often seen as a way of being different, immersing self in teenage culture and coming to believe that the opinion of anyone over the age of 25 is irrelevant. Thinking around the twenty-first-century church, there are few traditional denominations that are actually widely offering anything suitable for teenagers. We tend to expect them to conform to our church norms, enjoy doing the things we enjoy. It's probably fair to say that most churches have very few if any teens who regularly attend. These are the times when children begin to make decisions for themselves and many decide that church isn't for them. Whether this is connected to their peer group, the learning about different faiths at school or just because the church doesn't offer anything that is attractive to them is a moot point (actually it's probably a combination of all three along with many other factors). The question remains, how can the church actively speak into the situations of this generation?

Preparations

As in session 1. The verse of Lord of all Hopefulness to be

used this week is a new verse and can be found in the Worship Materials chapter.

Welcome (10 mins)

Question: The 1993 film Groundhog Day starring Bill Murray is based on the premise of a man living the same day again and again! If you could choose a day in your life to relive again, even just once, which one would you choose and why? (If everyone is choosing births/marriages, refine the question to say 'other than births/marriages/moments of coming to faith etc.'.)

Question: Can anyone name a day they would live differently the second time around?

Link: These are possibly very easy questions for some to answer and the obvious answers of births, marriages etc., have probably been in your heads. For others, this is probably a very hard question, maybe because there have been so many good days or maybe because there have been so few! I don't know if this question would be easier for an older or a younger person. Life is about choices though. Along the way of our journey through this mortal coil, we constantly make choices (or choices are made for us). Another film which plays on this 'choice' issue is Sliding Doors (1998) which is based on the premise of two parallel universes 'created' when someone either catches a train or misses it. Some people agonise about what problems making different choices will make in the long-term and often try to avoid making any changes at all. Others seem to be able to make decisions with no worries about long- or short-term future, simply choosing what is best in the here and now.

Neighbour: How easy do you find it to make choices? Why (no plenary)?

Link: The theme of choices is as relevant in the teenage years as any other time of life. In many countries, around the age of 14, teenagers take their 'Options', selecting which subjects to take through to formal examinations around age 16. Other choices will already have been talked through either by the child, the parents or jointly, e.g., which High School to attend, who to be friends with, and whether homework is a battle or not! Along the way we all make bad choices in friendship, in education, in relationships; the question is what the church has to say in these situations.

Worship (10 mins)

Link: We have moved from the early morning of our lives into 'elevensies' (and there's lots of choice there – tea or coffee, cake or biscuits! For many Western traditions of church, this is the time of Confirmation, when we make a public statement of our choice to follow Christ, even if the choice is more to keep people in our families and our churches happy because it's the thing to do! Our worship today focuses on the mid-morning, a time of 'self-discovery' as seen in the liturgies of Iona or Daily Personal Devotions.

Worship: Choose and use the relevant liturgy for your session – see the Worship Materials chapter. Use the 'Session 2' verse of Lord of all Hopefulness, a new verse written specially for these studies.

Pray: Opening Prayer.

Read: Psalm 119:105–112.

Pray: Prayer giving thanks for times of learning.

Read or sing: Lord of all Hopefulness – Session 2 verse in the Worship Materials chapter.

Pray: Lord's Prayer.

Pray: Closing Prayer leading into the session.

Word (40 mins)

Question: We begin each session with 'Word play' – using word association. What is the first word that comes into your mind when you hear the following words: teenager, exams, first kiss, emotions. What other words for those teenage years of life would you use?

Link: The teenage years are a great challenge to everyone with many people being able to share in later life how they suffered a 'teenage blip'! It is a time when you feel as if you are the only one who is feeling like this. Scientifically the brain is doing a similar rewire as when we are toddlers. The teenage years are effectively the 'terrible twos' with bigger 'children' and much more colourful and hurtful language.[1] Yet the teenage years can have some wonderful moments too.

Neighbour: Were your teenage years good? Try to share wonderful as well as horrendous moments (no plenary).

Link: And so, we head back to the words of Gary Barlow as he reflects on 'small town girls', the emotion of falling in love or just standing watching others going through this time. As you listen, reflect on what it is like to be a teenager today.

Play: Track 6 'Small Town Girls'.

Neighbour: Thinking about the lyrics of the song and the theme of 'choices' and the teenage years, what are your reflections?

Plenary.

Question: If the song were written about 'small town boys' what lyrics would have been included?

Question: Is the song a real reflection on teenage years?

Link: The teenage years are surrounded by choices and learning and society is geared to enabling each of us, as we pass through these life-defining times, to find our direction in life. The next 'I am' saying is all about enabling each of us, teenage or not, to find our direction through the lit pathway God is showing us, if we will only open our eyes. Today's readings are taken from quite a long passage about having open eyes which begins at the beginning of John chapter 7 as Jesus goes to the Feast of Tabernacles in Jerusalem and the people try to work out who Jesus is. The section continues right through to the end of John chapter 9 when Jesus talks about spiritual blindness. We're using two extracts from the middle of this long section.

Read: John 8:12–20, 9:1–7.

Question: What do you know about the Jewish Feast of Tabernacles?

Link: Tabernacles or 'Booths' is the feast of Sukkot, held between late September and late October, dependant on the Jewish lunar calendar. It is a seven-day holiday, a sort of harvest festival but also a festival of ingathering. It was one of the three annual pilgrimage festivals during which Jews were required, if they could, to make a pilgrimage to the Temple. During the festival, as a reminder of the itinerant nature of their forefathers in the Exodus, the Jews build 'Sukkot' or booths to eat and sometimes sleep in. In Jesus' day it was also a festival of light, when large golden candlesticks were lit in the Temple and the walls were lit up with great lights.

Question: Why do you think Jesus was focusing on the light?

Link: There's something of a parable here as Jesus is trying to show that, if they opened their eyes to his light, the Pharisees would see who Jesus was.

Question: Why do the Pharisees focus on the invalidity of Jesus' testimony (look at v13,17,18)?

Link: In Jewish courts in the first century, testimony required the validation by another reputable source.

Question: Why does Jesus refer to his Father as his other source (think here about the relationship between God and Jesus)?

Question: What passages from the Bible would the Pharisees think of when Jesus spoke of light?

Link: In Genesis 1, light is the first thing to be created by God and it's worth noting here the link that John has already made in 1:1–5 about how 'The Word' was with God, through him all things were created and how the light shines in the darkness![2]

Question: Is light always good?

Link: If you have ever cleaned a room and then had the sun to shine in, you instantly see how dirty it still is. Light is always good but it can be disconcerting as it shows up the imperfections we leave behind.

Question: Take a look at chapter 8 verses 24–26, what is your reaction to these verses, particularly in the context of Jesus speaking of light?

Link: v24–26 are difficult verses but they do indicate we have a choice to walk in Jesus' light or to walk our own way. Both ways having different consequences but where does John chapter 9 fit in? Here we have a direct play out of the conversation Jesus has just had.

Question: What is your reaction to the disciples' question in 9:2?

Question: Who are the really blind ones Jesus is speaking of?

Link: Jesus makes an interesting but challenging observation about how the day is for work but night is coming! This could easily be linked to the crucifixion but the challenge is how we link this to our everyday lives and those of people around us. The passage ends with the healing at the Pool of Siloam. Siloam interestingly means 'sent' – sometimes to find the light we need to go where we are sent.

Neighbour: How do you follow the light of Jesus as you walk in the way you are sent by him (no plenary)?

Witness (15 mins)

Link: The collect for the Second Sunday of Advent in the Book of Common Prayer calls on Christians to 'read, mark, learn and inwardly digest' God's word. One of the best ways of knowing God's light is to read his word. There is a strong link here with Psalm 119 which speaks of 'a lamp to our feet and a light to our path' but following isn't just about reading but doing.

Question: How does this work with people who know nothing of the Bible? How can we engage people beyond the walls of our churches with something they often see as a musty, old, irrelevant book? What are we offering? How is our offering perceived?

Neighbour: Why is the world so dark today? Is this the 'coming darkness' Jesus spoke of?

Plenary.

Link: Our second track today from Gary Barlow's album is a slightly unusual choice. This song was written as if it were his stillborn daughter Poppy speaking but could easily be read as someone struggling with a teenage love breakup, life problems and so on. As you listen think of those struggling with teenage issues at this time and reflect on what God is calling the church to do to help.

Play: Track 2 'Let Me Go'.

Worship: Space to reflect in silence.

Pray.

Session 3 – Love and Marriage

Background notes

After dealing with the early years of life, we now have three studies on different parts of adult life – love, faith and crisis! We begin with love. The teenage times of falling in and out of love graduate eventually for many into a never-ending search for love. One of the fastest growing areas of business in the technological age is dating apps and websites, each purportedly guaranteeing to have better algorithm and logic than all the others. People are searching for love and twenty-first-century society still finds it quite odd for someone to declare that they are happy and single. Marriage rates in the UK have stabilised in the last couple of years, although we are still at nearly an all-time low after a 40-year decline.[1] Interestingly the rate of divorce continues to increase rapidly, particularly among older generations (so called 'silver splitters'), so what does the church have to say to a society which is so driven by sexual imagery in its advertising and on TV, and who finds love as a commodity which can almost be bought and thrown away when circumstances change?

Preparations

As in session 1.

Welcome (10 mins)

Question: Which would you choose – a beautiful house and an ugly car or an ugly house and a beautiful car. Everyone has to choose, and saying you don't care for either isn't a choice – 'neither' or 'both' isn't one of the options here!

Link: I wonder how many of you struggled to answer the opening question as actually these things don't matter to you. We are thinking today about love and marriage (not as in the famous Sinatra song though!). For some love and marriage is something that can be picked up, bought, used and thrown away almost as something which doesn't matter. You only need to look at some of the stories in the tabloid magazines about 'celebrities' to see this. Some would even say that 'love' itself is the problem, particularly in the form of marriage, as it is outdated, patriarchal and unbalanced. And yet there are those who fall in love and for whom the whole world changes.

Question: What is love?

Link: We do need to all be aware that, for some, this is a difficult issue and not all are called to a life of partnership but to a life of singleness. But it is an important stage of life for us to work out what the church's response should be to those who have chosen to be devoted to another person i.e. in marriage.

Worship (10 mins)

Link: We have moved to noon, the 'pinnacle' of the day. The obvious link here is in the marriage ceremonies but there are many traditions which have liturgies for noontime. Our worship today focuses on the mid-point of the day, a time to pause and reflect before the afternoon begins, echoed in worship for noon from the liturgies of the Northumbria Community or the Episcopal Church's Noonday Prayers.

Worship: Choose either the worship structure listed below or use a relevant resource for the noon of the day, some options are listed in the Worship Materials chapter. Use verse 2 of Lord of all Hopefulness which speaks of the noon of the day.

Pray: Opening Prayer.

Read: Psalm 24.

Pray: Prayer giving thanks for God's love.

Read or sing: Lord of all Hopefulness v2.

Pray: Lord's Prayer.

Pray: Closing Prayer leading into the session.

Word (40 mins)

Question: We begin each session with 'Word play' – using word association. What is the first word that comes into your mind when you hear the following words: wedding, love, singleness, Valentines. What other words for this season of life would you use?

Link: We move from the 'age-specific/time-specific' studies for our next three sessions, to ones which cover different aspects of adult life.

Question: Finish this sentence 'Love is …'.

Link: Lots of pop songs have love as a theme, whether falling in and out or being in love, and Gary Barlow's album is no different. Our first song today is about how we like to love.

Play: Track 8 'We Like to Love'.

Neighbour: Thinking about the lyrics of the song and the theme of 'love' what are your reflections?

Plenary.

Question: Do we really like to love? Why?

Question: What are some Biblical examples of love (worth making a link here to the cross)?

Link: Someone once said that the Bible is God's love letter to us and there are so many images of that love. Today's 'I am' sayings are some of those images. Note today we have two 'I am' sayings which are so intrinsically linked.

Read: John 10:1–21.

Question: Describe a shepherd.

Question: Is your image a twenty-first- or a first-century one?

Link: Shepherds in the first century were certainly not meek, lamb-cuddling, whistling and sheep-dog directing folk, they were often very strong people. Commentators have even referred to them as the bodybuilders of their day! Their lives involved struggles with wild beasts, lifting and carrying sheep, guarding the entrances to the flock (e.g., gate) and also regularly performing acts of immense courage. Through this the flock would have known their shepherd and the shepherd would have known the sheep by name, even raising them almost as children.

Question: Where else in the Bible would you find shepherds (try and think about Old and New Testament images here)?

Question: Are these all positive images?

Link: There are many images of shepherds in the Bible, many of which are negative.

Read: Ezekiel 34:1–10.

Question: At what time in the life of Israel was the prophet Ezekiel active?

Link: Ezekiel was active during the years of the fall of the Assyrian Empire to Babylon under Nebuchadnezzar and the subsequent siege and fall of Jerusalem, the beginning of the Exile for the southern kingdom of Judah.

Question: How are the leaders acting?

Question: What is the image of a shepherd defining here?

Link: Shepherd was often an image reserved for the leaders of the nation, those who were shepherding the flock of people and Ezekiel is hugely critical of what the leaders of the day were doing.

Question: Heading back into the John 10 reading, what does Jesus mean when he says he is the gate?

Link: This is all about protection of the flock. The sheep in the fold would have been protected by the shepherd physically lying across the entrance. A hired hand would flee at the first sign of a problem as the sheep weren't theirs and a thief wouldn't use the gate at all. Both the thief and the hired hand were interested in the sheep for their own sake, only the shepherd had the sheep first in mind. They were prepared to sacrifice themselves voluntarily.

Question: When do the sheep become part of the flock?

Question: In terms of first-century shepherds, the sheep were born or bought into the flock but apply the same question to Christ's flock, when and how do sheep become part of Christ's flock? How are they accepted?

Question: What does it mean for Jesus to be our shepherd?

Link: Jesus being the gate and the shepherd is for the sheep's benefit not for his. He is there to serve them, to look after them, to ensure they are safe.

Question: What do the words in v8 mean to you? Who are the 'other voices'?

Neighbour: What 'other voices' have you heard? Did you follow them or not?

Plenary.

Question: The sheep know the shepherd according to v15 so how do we know Jesus' voice?

Link: The other sheep that Jesus is speaking of in this passage are probably the Gentiles, remembering that he is speaking to Jews at this point not Christians, but in all cases it is about following the shepherd not for our own good but for his sake. We need to allow ourselves to be guided by him.

Neighbour: When you come to church do you come for what you can get out of it, out of God himself, or are you allowing the shepherd of the sheep to guide you?

Plenary.

Witness (15 mins)

Link: Possibly some of the most famous words from the Marriage service are 'till death us do part', something that couples coming to be wed truly mean. They speak out of love and yet we know that so many marriages today do not last until death parts them. This is the state we find in twenty-first-century Western society. Marriage celebrations are one of the key rites of passage where the church is involved in people's lives and yet so many people 'use' churches simply because they will look nice on the photos. Surely the church has more to offer to people than picturesque settings?

Question: What does the church have to offer people that will help them in their relationships?

Link: The best example of relationship is in the Good Shepherd who lays down his life for his sheep. Any relationship has to have at its heart a concern for the other person before self. Jesus is our example of good relationships but it requires us to fully trust his way and also to remember to be glad.

Question: Verse 16 reminds us that the sheep know the shepherd and are one flock. How often does your church divide and give off the sense that life is joyless, overbusy and pleasureless under the shadow of him?

Link: Surely the shepherd who enables us to 'not want', who 'leads us beside still waters' and who 'restores our souls' and who 'sets before us a banquet in the presence of our enemies',[2] wouldn't want his sheep to be joyless, overbusy and pleasureless. As we listen to our second track from Gary Barlow which speaks of a love that will go thousands of miles for a possible moment of meeting, maybe we need to reflect on our relationship with God and how we should truly act as his sheep.

Play: Track 7 '6th Avenue'.

Worship: Space to reflect in silence.

Pray.

Session 4 – Lost and Found

Background notes

I wonder if you have ever been on a walk with someone become distracted, maybe by an incredible view, for a brief moment, so when you look up those you are with have gone! Not a nice feeling. We're not often well and truly lost; we often have a basic idea of at least the town or village we are in but to be totally lost, no map, no compass, not knowing which way to turn! It can be like being in a maze with everywhere looking the same and lots of dead ends. In our postmodern age where there is no metanarrative, no overarching story, it is interesting to note the explosion of 'spiritualties' which are designed to help each person search for their own meaning of life. The search for meaning and purpose in life has gone on for centuries and there have been many along the way who have come forward with ideas of an answer – the most ironic of all these could be seen in Douglas Adams' work when his characters discover the answer is the number 42 and then have to go on a journey to find out what the question was![1] We all have spiritual journeys and the answer to our faith questions may not be 42 but, at some point in their life, everyone questions the existence of God, even if for a brief moment. This is obviously a topic which inherently involves the church and, as Christians, we should be good at helping people on this journey, meeting them at the heavenly lost and found; the question is how good we actually are at doing this and if, as Christians, we need to learn how to do it better.

Preparations

As in session 1.

Welcome (10 mins)

Question: What is the most valuable thing you have ever lost (valuable in any sense)?

Link: We live in a society that is so busy that we regularly lose things. We misplace keys (although some people have those key rings which will sing when you whistle so you can find them), our phones, our remote controls. A lot of this is because we simply have far too much stuff. In recent years the BBC have produced programmes where families are taken 'back in time' as their house was remodelled as if it were, say, in the 1950s and they were so surprised at how little there was in the house.[2] We have, over time, continually increased the amount of junk that we surround ourselves with, all in the name of making our lives easier of course and, because we have so much junk, we seem to have become better at losing it. Recently a train-operator in the UK revealed some of the things that had been left behind (or lost and found) on their trains – they included a wooden casket containing someone's ashes, a framed picture of the British cooking sensation Mary Berry, eight sets of false teeth, a live hamster, a bag of haggis, a Barry Manilow CD and a 6ft inflatable dinosaur![3]

Question: Are you the sort of person who regularly misplaces things?

Link: Some people seem to be better at losing things than others – and this can stretch into the mental (losing one's marbles!) and spiritual worlds too (finding and losing faith). Doubt is one of the biggest players in this market and, as we are surrounded by so many spiritual options, it's easy to see why people can find themselves drifting with no particular destination. Today's study is another 'season' of adulthood (rather than an age of life), focusing on whether as Christians we need to become better at helping people to discover the God who loves them.

Worship (10 mins)

Link: We head into the afternoon of life, moments of relaxing and daydreaming, to have time to see what the possibilities are. This is a time to try out different spiritualties and think in new ways, allowing ourselves to be renewed or even having the space to just state that nothing has changed since the morning of our lives. Our worship today is for the afternoon and focuses on the reflection space offered by the afternoon mirrored in the liturgies of Methodist Christian Renewal or BCP Evensong.

Worship: Choose either the worship structure listed below or use a relevant resource for the afternoon of the day, some options are listed in the Worship Materials chapter. Use verse 3 of Lord of all Hopefulness which speaks of the eve of the day.

Pray: Opening Prayer.

Read: Luke 1:46–55.

Pray: Prayer giving thanks for all God's goodness.

Read or sing: Lord of all Hopefulness v3.

Pray: Lord's Prayer.

Pray: Closing Prayer leading into the session.

Word (40 mins)

Question: We begin each session with 'Word play' – using word association. What is the first word that comes into your mind when you hear the following words: faith, hope, trust, knowledge. What other words for the searching times of life would you use?

Question: Describe what it feels like to be lost?

Neighbour: Have you or anyone you know ever been spiritually lost?

Plenary.

Link: Being lost can be a very uncomfortable place to be and yet some people seem able to live lives which can be seen from the outside to be totally lost, and yet they seem oblivious.

Question: List some ways you know people have found faith?

Link: One of the most powerful songs on Gary Barlow's album is simply entitled 'God'. Gary doesn't profess to be a person of faith but has said in interviews that he prays. Through the words of this song there seems to be a definite element of searching but also challenge for those who have already found God.

Play: Track 5 'God'.

Neighbour: Thinking about the lyrics of the song and the theme of 'lost and found' what are your reflections?

Plenary.

Neighbour: Describe your faith journey, particularly noting times when you have been lost and found (no plenary).

Link: There are many stories in the Bible about being lost and found, Jesus' parables in Luke 15 being some of the most obvious ones. The song 'God' has a great challenge in it though which reminds us that being lost is one thing, actually not showing people the way is another! Today's passage is a challenging one and also possibly one of the most well-known sections of scripture, partly because of its inclusion in the Funeral service liturgies of many Christian denominations. We need to remember as we hear this reading that as the disciples listen to Jesus speak, we are pre-crucifixion and they have all just shared the Passover together, and in the verse before we begin, Judas has just left to betray Jesus.

Read: John 13:31–14:14.

Link: The first thing we need to note about this passage is the continuing theme of Jesus as the Good Shepherd to his disciples (14:1–4) which we spoke about in Session 3. Jesus is again offering himself as a voluntary sacrifice and Peter would like to offer to do the same (even though at this point he hasn't fully grasped what all this means) (13:37–38).

Question: Are you impulsive like Peter, puzzled like Thomas or questioning like Philip?

Link: Jesus offers his disciples assurance (they have seen him and known him) and peace (or shalom) – this is particularly noted when you add the rest of the chapter or at least v27 which is often included at funerals.

Question: Why are the questions/statements that Peter,

39

Thomas and Philip ask/make wrong?

Question: Peter is almost unthinking. Thomas wants proof. Philip is too pre-occupied with the here and now. Why?

Link: We need to remember the circumstances here. It is so easy, particularly with such a familiar passage to forget the context. We are on Maundy Thursday evening; the disciples and Jesus have been in Jerusalem under growing threat from the Jewish religious leaders; they've eaten the Passover together and Jesus has washed their feet (as a servant would do) and then told them one of them would betray him. No wonder with all this that they are slightly 'spooked'. Jesus then tells them he's leaving them!

Question: Does this help to explain the disciples' behaviour and questions?

Link: Jesus goes on to say he won't show them the way, he is the way (the restorer of relationships with God); he is the truth (the conduit of confession); he is the life (as God intended it to be). Remember Christians were first known as 'Followers of the Way' probably with links to Jesus' statement here in John 14.

Question: If we were called 'Followers of the Way' in twenty-first-century Britain, rather than Christians, what would be different?

Link: The concept of 'The Way' brings to mind images of itinerancy, people on a journey to a new promised land, even picking up the theme in 1 Peter 2:11 where we are urged to live as 'temporary residents'.[4]

Question: 'I am the way ... no one comes to the Father except through me' sounds like a very difficult statement in a pluralistic, postmodern society. How can we square this circle?

Link: This statement might seem narrow, even out-of-date, but Jesus doesn't say 'the church is the only way', he says he is.

Question: Does this statement make a difference to our view of Jesus' claim here?

Neighbour: Do you feel the church sometimes claims a

monopoly on the way to God? Is this right or wrong?

Plenary.

Question: Is there a difference between tolerance and equality?

Link: Many commentators today struggle with Jesus' claim here but there are echoes of this throughout the New Testament. Our pluralistic society will regularly push equality which can, in some cases, water down God's message into an almost puerile, inoffensive mash. Just before the reference to 'temporary residents', Peter, in his first letter, notes that Jesus is a stone to make people stumble,[5] the Greek word being σκανδαλον (scandalon). Jesus here doesn't claim to be a version of the truth but he is the truth – note Paul's statement on Christ in Colossians 1 as the 'image of the invisible God'.[6]

Neighbour: What difference does all this make to your view of Jesus being the way, the truth and the life?

Plenary.

Witness (15 mins)

Link: The Great Litany of the Book of Common Prayer used before the Eucharist has the most fantastic prayers:

From all inordinate and sinful affections; and from all the deceits of the world, the flesh, and the devil, Good Lord, deliver us. From all false doctrine, heresy, and schism; from hardness of heart, and contempt of thy Word and commandment, Good Lord, deliver us.[7]

In our postmodern, pluralistic society it would be easy to see these prayers as almost seeking ways to avoid contact but we are also called to be a people who help others to find their way to Christ.

Question: What does your church actively do to encourage people to find Christ?

Neighbour: What have you personally done in the last 12

months as part of this mission work of your church (no plenary)?

Link: Many churches run courses such as Alpha and encourage members to bring people they know to 'seeker-style' services but actually one of the greatest things we can do as Christians is to simply tell others. Jesus spoke of his followers doing greater things – including miracles but also telling people all over the world not just first-century Palestine.

Question: Jesus says that he will do whatever we ask in his name[8] – are these 'magic words'?

Link: Asking for things in Jesus' name is about seeking his will. If we are seeking his will, we will only ask for things he wants (remember the WWJD wristbands of the 1990s).

Question: If Gary Barlow came and asked you 'have you found God?', what is the way to find him? What would your answer be?

Link: Much of Gary's writing on this album seems to have come from the crisis in his life after the breakup of *Take That* in the 1990s and his searching. Our final song today is part of that searching but also the way he has found peace in who he is. As you listen, reflect on how your journey has been but also how this can help us as we seek to help others to find themselves in God.

Play: Track 9 'Since I saw you last'.

Worship: Space to reflect in silence.

Pray.

Session 5 – Crises and Counselling

Background notes

We live in an age where mental health is, thankfully, slightly better understood and some of this comes from the recognition that there is a long way to go on this. We have moved from the days where people spent lives locked up in asylums (although many people are still sectioned for long periods of time even today) and yet the mind remains one of the most mysterious parts of the human body. Although we can learn about its physiology, there are still only theories about how memory and decision-making actually work. There's a lot on the web about electrical impulses and the hippocampus but whereas we've been doing heart transplants since 1967, there's no sign yet of brain transplants. As a result of the 'discovery' of the huge variety of mental health issues that people can face, particularly exacerbated by the immediacy 'required' in the technological age, which actually only seems to increase stress, there has been an explosion of different techniques: mindfulness, CBT, even an encouragement for people to be personality-profiled using the many models available. 'Rehab' and counselling, which at one time would have been a guilty secret, have become something to almost boast about – a badge of honour! In the midst of this challenging background, what does the church have to say to people who come in moments of crisis?

Preparations

As in session 1.

Welcome (10 mins)

Question: When Richard Bacon was a presenter on BBC Radio 5 Live, he had a weekly 'moan-in' with the best moan of the week being given the title 'Moaner Lisa'! Each moan was scored out of ten for content and passion – all were trivial things such as people parking in toddler spaces etc. Now it's your turn – what in life drives you crazy? The rest of us will mark you out of ten!

Link: We do like a good moan don't we! And, actually, many of us spend our lives moaning about the things we have and the things we don't have, the people we meet, the people and situations that get on our nerves and even life itself. Many of the things we moan about are trivial but there are times in all our lives when things can become more serious and, as they do, each of us copes in a different way. Some people are able to muddle through whereas others find themselves in the middle of a crisis. Counsellors will tell you that all of us are susceptible in times of crisis. It can be our personality, the form the crisis takes and even the people we have around us that can help us to cope. Our study today encourages us to think about the crises of life and to reflect on how as Christians we should be there to help others in their times of need.

Worship (10 mins)

Link: We head into the evening of life, the time of day when many people sit down and reflect on the things that have happened. Sitting and thinking can be a good thing to do as it gives us the opportunity to place all our ups and downs before God. Our worship today is based using liturgical styles that are intended to be reflective in nature and used as evening approaches, e.g., Taizé or Episcopal Church BCP Vespers.

Worship: Choose either the worship structure listed below or use a relevant resource for the evening of the day, some options are listed in the Worship Materials chapter. Use the 'Session 5' verse of Lord of all Hopefulness, a new verse written specially for these studies.

Pray: Opening Prayer.

Read: Matthew 5:14–16, 2 Corinthians 4:5–6, Psalm 139:10–11.

Pray: Prayer giving thanks for hope in times of crises.

Read or sing: Lord of all Hopefulness – Session 5 verse in the Worship Materials chapter.

Pray: Lord's Prayer.

Pray: Closing Prayer leading into the session.

Word (40 mins)

Question: We begin each session with 'Word play' – using word association. What is the first word that comes into your mind when you hear the following words: midlife crisis, ageing, retirement, crisis. What other words for the crisis times of life would you use?

Link: Everyone has problem times in their lives; some seem to have more problems than others and some cope with problems better than others. Before we begin to head deeper into this subject, it is worth noting that it is something which may touch people deeply, so please do care for yourselves and for each other in this session. Everyone has problems and we could be in the middle of them now or this session could rake up things that are long buried. This is a safe space. Anything shared here must be kept confidential.

Neighbour: Reflect on a time of crisis (big or small is fine) with your neighbour (no plenary).

Link: Beginning with reflection on our own problems puts us in the position of noting that we all live with issues – no one is immune. It is about how we find a way through them that is important. Sometimes, for many, simply finding where to begin can be extremely challenging. Meanwhile, one of the traits of times of crises is to put on a brave face. Our first Gary Barlow track today is an incredibly powerful song that speaks about how we often portray ourselves as being perfectly okay whilst we're dying inside.

Play: Track 11 'Dying inside'.

Neighbour: Thinking about the lyrics of the song and the theme of 'crisis and counselling' what are your reflections?

Plenary.

Link: Finding someone to help in the difficult times is vital, someone to carry the load whilst we are struggling on. For Christians, the imagery of the famous *Footprints* poem is an important one as we realise just how important God can be as we walk through the tough times of life. Many people, who have had successful counselling, will tell you just how important the special relationship is with the counsellor – someone who just knows. Someone with whom you can just be yourself!

Question: What is it like to be in a time of crisis? What are the emotions?

Link: One of the strongest emotions those in deep crisis can feel is a sense of feeling lost. We could be encountering those who are spiritually lost, but many people who come to find help from the church at times like this are simply needing some emotional support. To ask them 'Do you know Jesus?' could seem a bit trite and extremely uncaring!

Question: So how does this link to Jesus' statement about him being the Vine and us the branches, our 'I am' saying for today?

Link: This 'I am' saying is different from the others we will study in this series. The other 'I am' sayings are all about who Jesus is for us – our bread, our light, our way and so on. This saying is more about us, our connection with him and also how important it is that we remain there.

Read: John 15:1–17.

Link: The reading's context is similar to that of our last session. We're in that time between the Last Supper and Jesus' arrest in Gethsemane. Many commentators speculate that, on the journey to the garden, Jesus and his disciples might have either passed through a vineyard or even simply seen the vine carvings that were on the Temple walls which symbolised the 'vine' of Israel. Whatever the actual situation was, the vine was something that was a hugely important image to all first-century Jews. The vine was about life, the life of the nation. The Old Testament is full of vine references, e.g., passages such as Jeremiah 2:21 and Hosea 10:1 use this imagery.

Read: Isaiah 5:1–7.

Question: What sort of fruit is the vine producing?

Link: Isaiah, among other prophets, is keen to note that the vine isn't producing the fruit that God wants or had planned. In God's eyes, the vine, the people of Israel, have a purpose, which is to produce the fruit that God intends.

Question: Looking back to the John passage, what is the purpose of the vine itself?

Link: The vine is the lifeforce. Without the vine, the branches would be unsupported, lifeless and unfruitful. The vine is there to produce nourishment.

Question: Why and how are vines pruned today?

Link: Vines are pruned to encourage better growth. In the spring, vines are often savagely pruned back to a point where they can look almost dead, but within weeks they are sprouting new, succulent and sustainable growth.

Question: What do the branches provide for the vine?

Link: The branches provide a platform for growth, for leaves which give the plant even more life, and fruit. Branches without growth are pointless. The vine without branches is also pointless – both are important to each other.

Question: Does this mean that the created are important to the Creator?

Link: We need here to link to Genesis 2 and remind ourselves of the personal relationship that God created us to have with him, a relationship that we have soured regularly but that the Creator continually seeks to restore.

Question: Is it a 'nice' relationship between vine and branches?

Link: The branches and the vine are interdependent but it is up to the Creator to prune us.

Question: What would it mean to be pruned as Christians?

Question: Does this mean that God causes bad things to

happen to us?

Question: How do we respond to those who feel pruned and thrown into the fire?

Witness (15 mins)

Link: In the baptism liturgy in the Book of Common Prayer, the priest announces that 'this child is regenerate and grafted into the body'.[1] There is also something here to be said for those who have not been part of the vine but are now finding the touch of God on their lives.

Question: Does this phrase help us to think about those who are 'thrown into the fire'?

Link: Often the links with the community around us at times of crisis is through personal contact. As Christians, it is important that we recognise that, as John Wesley once put it, 'the Bible knows nothing of solitary religion',[2] i.e. we need each other but, also we need to note how important it is that others know of our faith. There have been stories doing the rounds on social media in recent years about Christians taking the step of sitting in a coffee shop once a week with a sign offering 'free prayer'. This may seem a little extreme to us but we need to be ready to help all in need and often the people we are called to help are those whom we know already.

Question: In what ways does the church you attend seek to help people in times of need?

Neighbour: In what ways are you part of this vital work of the church (no plenary)?

Link: We might feel wholly inappropriate and unable to help in anyway but it is important to just learn to listen to both the person and to God and allow God to do the healing and grafting! Pruning can hurt, it can cause our branches to bleed but the cuts can allow us to grow. We need to be people who stand beside others as they seek God's hand on their lives; as Gary Barlow puts it in our final song, we need to be other people's heroes.

During Gary's darkest times it was another singer/songwriter who kept faith in him and supported him[3] and it is Elton with whom he duets on this song – listen to the way that Gary actually speaks about Elton John in the lyrics of this song and reflect on how we need to be that for others.

Play: Track 4 'Face to Face'.

Worship: Space to reflect in silence.

Pray.

Session 6 – Life and Death

Background notes

It is the one inevitability of life – at some point, each and every one of us is going to die. That may seem like a morbid statement but it is true. The world of philosophy is full of people defining what death is and also what happens after we die. One of the privileges of ministry is the opportunity to share with families in the days after they have lost a loved one and so many have commented on the wonderful nature of the Christian hope that the church offers. I have lost count of the number of times I have been asked where their loved one is now by those who are proud to share with me that they are atheists on my arrival for the funeral visit. The concept of death being the absolute end with nothing beyond is, for many, a thought too scary to perceive but they may also find the notion of heaven far-fetched. For Christians death isn't the end; it's the beginning of a new phase of our lives. In 1975 Elisabeth Kubler-Ross, an American doctor, wrote a seminal book based on her experiences of dealing with death called, *Death: the final stage of growth* – a title which many have found helpful as they have tried to come to terms with difficult times of grief. Yet, to me, this title also reminds me that death is about life – it is a final stage of growing. Growth can hurt, as many children and teenagers will tell you when they experience growing pains (never mind the emotion trauma of the terrible twos and the teenage years), but it is also about a continuation of life. Life is for living and, when pushed, many people are more scared of the process of dying (the pain and suffering they may endure) rather than death itself. As Christians we treasure life before and after death and this final study provides space for us to focus on how we can engage with people beyond our walls at times of joy and sorrow.

Preparations

As in session 1.

Welcome (10 mins)

Question: Apart from Jesus, who do you wish you could have met who died before you were born and why?

Question: Does anyone ever wish they could 'pop back' to a different era in life, maybe one that was before you were born to see how people lived? If so, to when and why?

Link: All around us, all the time, is life and death. They say that every second four babies are born and two people die.[1] Once we are born, the one inevitability of our lives, the one thing we all share, is that one day we will die. That might seem like a very morbid statement but it is true. Today's study is deliberately entitled life and death because although death is inevitable, we need to recognise that life is important to live to the full.

Neighbour: Share with your neighbour your feelings about death – is it something you struggle with? Why (no plenary)?

Link: Today's study is another one where we could find ourselves full of emotion from current times in our lives, but it could also bring back things from the past which we found difficult. We do need to protect ourselves and care for each other as we discuss. The passage we will share today shows Jesus full of emotion too, struggling with loss. As we look at this season of life, we need to remember how much we are all touched with loss and think about how as church we can engage with people more at these most difficult times of life.

Worship (10 mins)

Link: We head to the end of the day, a time when sleep overcomes us and we hand our safety over to the God who never sleeps.[2] Our worship today reminds us of liturgies created to surround us with hope and love at the end of the days – the Methodist Prayer in the Evening or Episcopal Church BCP Compline.

Worship: Choose either the worship structure listed below or use a relevant resource for the evening of the day, some options are listed in the Worship Materials chapter. Use verse 4 of Lord of all Hopefulness which speaks of the end of the day.

Pray: Opening Prayer.

Read: Isaiah 40:27–31.

Pray: Prayer giving thanks for God's care through the night.

Read or sing: Lord of all Hopefulness v4.

Pray: Lord's Prayer.

Pray: Closing Prayer.

Word (40 mins)

Question: We begin each session with 'Word play' – using word association. What is the first word that comes into your mind when you hear the following words: life, funeral, wake, death. What other words for the end times of life would you use?

Link: In the twenty-first-century, death is almost a taboo subject. But it has also been trivialised by video games where it is so easy to shoot others and made almost irrelevant as there are no consequences. It is serialised and dramatized by soap operas and Hollywood. Yet death is something that many struggle to talk about. I wonder how many people thought twice about this study knowing the subject matter! Even Christians struggle to talk about death and often use poems at funerals to try and engage with the subject matter with phrases such as 'I am in the next room'[3] which some people find helpful and others want to shout 'well come back then!'.

Neighbour: What is the most comfortable way, if any, for you to talk about death?

Plenary.

Link: For many people the easiest way to deal with death is through an ironic humour. The British comedian Victoria Wood once spoke of the difference between Indian funerals and British ones saying that in Indian ones the widow used to throw herself on the funeral pyre of her late husband whereas in Britain the widow simply hauls herself into the kitchen with her friends and says something like, '72 baps Connie, you slice, I'll spread!'.[4] Yes, it is ironic and funny but there is an inherent truth here – humour helps us to cope. Our first Gary Barlow track today makes light of the process of dying, the lyrics of the song are written as if someone who has died is speaking to the people coming to their funeral. There are some great links here with the 'I am' sayings, note the reference in the lyrics to the Lord's my Shepherd!

Play: Track 1 'Requiem'.

Neighbour: Thinking about the lyrics of the song and the theme of 'life and death', what are your reflections?

Plenary.

Link: We come to the seventh 'I am' saying today and we meet Jesus and see his humanity and his divinity proclaimed as he deals with the death of someone he was fond of. This is a long reading but it is worth having the context of the whole story.

Read: John 11:1–44.

Link: From our last study we've moved back earlier in the story of Jesus' life again. We're still in the final year of Jesus' life, but are now possibly in the last month or so before the journey to Jerusalem. Here we find one of Jesus' friends dying.

Question: What would the tomb have been like?

Question: Why did Jesus wait three days?

Link: It is worth noting at this point the Jewish customs surrounding death. In the heat of Israel, the funeral often took place the same day as the death because of quick decomposition. Tombs were often family affairs, dug into rock, places which were cool. The body would have been tightly wrapped in cloth and laid deep in the rock and a huge stone rolled across the mouth to stop grave robbers. The Jews believed that the soul used to hover over the body for three days after death before departing. It is also worth noting that just prior to this passage, the religious leaders have already tried to silence Jesus and are looking for another reason to try again.

Question: Martha speaks of the resurrection of the dead on the last day – was this commonly believed amongst the Jewish people of her day?

Link: We need here to note the difference between the Pharisees, who did believe in a form of life after death, and the Sadducees, who didn't.

Question: What do you think Martha was thinking when Jesus said he was the resurrection?

Question: Did Martha expect to see Lazarus again? If so, when?

Neighbour: Discuss the power of the words of John 11:35 – what does this say to you about Jesus?

Plenary.

Link: Jesus doesn't hide the emotion that comes with losing a friend but meets it head on.

Question: Where do we often hear the words of this 'I am' saying in church?

Link: The most common use is at the beginning of a funeral service as the person leading the coffin comes down the aisle quoting passages of scripture.

Question: Could this phrase be seen as almost insensitive? If so, how can we make it less so.

Link: In the passage from John, Jesus talks about being the resurrection and the life and Martha says, 'yes I believe it', but Jesus takes it a step further and says that they would see the power of those words, right now! There is a message here for all people that eternal life isn't something we just gain on death but that eternity begins now.

Question: If we are living in eternity now, describe it!

Question: What does Jesus mean by 'eternal life'?

Link: In the midst of the darkness of life which surrounds losing a loved one, Jesus is speaking of bringing a glimmer of light. Funerals are sad as we say 'see you soon' to someone but they should also be great moments of hope. Jesus speaks of eternity as being in a conscious, constant fellowship with him.

Question: So, what is the opposite?

Link: Over the centuries, people have tried to draw depictions of 'hell' but there is a great sense in this passage of this simply being eternal separation from God.

Read: Romans 8:38–39.

Question: How does this fit in with the passage from John?

Link: This is Paul at his most eloquent talking about how nothing, not even death, can separate us. Paul is saying that he's sure that the God who loves us so much in this life isn't going to let a little thing like death get in the way of that love. Easter Sunday morning puts this into context as we sing about how death has been defeated by Jesus.

Question: How can we talk about the life that Jesus has won in the face of the death that is inevitable to each of us?

Witness (15 mins)

Link: Possibly some of the most familiar words in the funeral liturgy begin 'ashes to ashes, dust to dust' but the next phrase is so important 'in sure and certain hope of the resurrection to eternal life, through our Lord Jesus Christ'.[5]

Question: How do you think the world around us sees these words?

Link: Often they are the words people don't want to hear and probably most very rarely reflect on the enormous promise contained in them. We see so many of our community at funerals, possibly more than at other moments in life and so many people see this as an opportunity to share the gospel message.

Question: What would you say to someone's family, who knew that the person who had died deliberately walked away from God, when they asked where you thought they were now?

Link: A difficult question but some would answer this by

saying that the Jesus of the gospels reveals to us on so many occasions that God is the God of another chance and who are we as mere humans to judge what God does.

Question: As we come to the end of these studies, what has been the greatest revelation to you about the 'I am' sayings?

Link: There has been and will be much to ponder on and we need to allow God to lead us into his way of thinking about life, about death and, as shown through the 'I am' sayings, who he is – we need, as Gary Barlow says in this final song to 'go ahead and jump!'.

Play: Track 3 'Jump'.

Worship: Space to reflect in silence.

Pray.

Worship Resources

Additional Verses for Lord of all Hopefulness

Session 2

Lord of all consciousness, Lord of all choice,
Whose words still direct us with powerful voice,
Be there at our learning, and give us, we pray,
Your wisdom and skill, Lord, in the morn of the day.

Session 5

Lord of all doubtfulness, Lord of all time,
Whose ears always listen to ramblings of mine,
Be there in our crises, and give us, we pray,
Your trust in our hearts, Lord, at the close of the day.

* * *

Further Ideas for Liturgies for use in Worship sections

Session 1 – Birth and Childhood

Methodist Worship Book Prayer in the Morning

Episcopal Church Book of Common Prayer Morning Prayer

Session 2 – Choices and Learning

Iona Morning Prayer liturgy

Episcopal Church Book of Common Prayer Daily Personal Devotions

Session 3 – Love and Marriage

Northumbria Community Noonday Prayer

Episcopal Church Book of Common Prayer Noonday Prayer

Session 4 – Lost and Found

Methodist Worship Book Act of Christian Renewal

Book of Common Prayer Evensong

Session 5 – Crises and Counselling

Taize Prayer for the Day

Episcopal Church Book of Common Prayer Vespers

Session 6 – Life and Death
Methodist Worship Book Prayer in the Evening
Episcopal Church Book of Common Prayer Compline

Author Biography

Ben Clowes is a Methodist Minister. He is married to Catherine and has two sons. His previous circuit in Cheshire included churches in both some of the wealthiest and most deprived parts of the country, serving both traditional church and a Fresh Expression situated in a Christian café. He is currently serving the church as a Superintendent Minister of a vibrant circuit in North Yorkshire. He is keen to encourage the church to seek new ways of connecting with wider society and showing how the Gospel is still as relevant today in our post-modern times as it has always been.

Note to reader

Thank you for purchasing *Since we saw you last*. These studies were obviously written with specific church communities and situations in mind. As such you may need to adapt to contextualise them for your own situation, whether you are using these with a group or for your own personal devotions. I am always thrilled to hear about ways in which these studies have been used and how they have helped people on their journey with God. For more information and to contact me please go to my Facebook page https://fb.me/BenClowesBooks . Please also visit this site for news of upcoming other works.

Appendix 1 – References

Introduction

1   See Abraham, W.J. (2005), *Wesley for Armchair Theologians*, p.111ff for a more detailed discussion.

2 Methodist Conference (2003), *His Presence Makes the Feast*, statement of the Conference on the Methodist Theology of Holy Communion paragraph 77.

3   Based on the hymn *And Can it Be* by Charles Wesley (1707–1788).

4   Moodie, C. (2013) Daily Mirror [Online]. Available at http://www.mirror.co.uk/3am/celebrity-news/gary-barlow-shedding-five-stone-2866963.

Background material

1   Brainy Quote (n.d.) Brainy Quote [Online]. Available at http://www.brainyquote.com/quotes/quotes/r/ramdass601695.html#0cRhFlH81p3mjpcf.99.

2   John 10:10 (NIV).

3   Ecclesiastes 1:2a (NIV).

4   Ecclesiastes 2:7 (NIV).

5   Philippians 2:6–7 (Living Bible).

6   John 1:1 (NIV).

7   Exodus 3:14 (NIV).

8   John 10:33 (NIV).

9   Mark 4:41 (NIV).

10   Matthew 21:10 (NIV).

11   John 8:25 (NIV).

12   John 4:26 (NRSV).

13   Stokes, W. (2018) The Frisky [Online]. Available at http://www.thefrisky.com/2014-03-19/new-study-figured-out-the-12-most-common-themes-of-musics-1-hits-in-the-past-50-years/.

14   Matthew 28:1-20 (NIV).

Session 1

1   Healey, J.G. (n.d.) Afriprov.org [Online]. Available at http://www.afriprov.org/african-proverb-of-the-month/23-1998proverbs/137-november-1998-proverb.html.
2   Church of England (n.d.) Church of England [Online]. Available at https://www.churchofengland.org/prayer-and-worship/worship-texts-and-resources/book-common-prayer/public-baptism-such-are-riper.

Session 2

1   Carey, T. (2015) The Telegraph [Online]. Available at http://www.telegraph.co.uk/news/health/children/11739219/Revealed-Inside-the-mind-of-a-teenager.html.
2   See John 1:1-5 (NIV).

Session 3

1   Evaluation of data on https://www.ons.gov.uk/people populationandcommunity/birthsdeathsandmarriages/marragecohabitationandcivilpartnerships/bulletins/marriagesinenglandandwalesprovisional/2015.
2   Psalm 23 (NIV).

Session 4

1   See Douglas Adams, *The Hitchhiker's Guide to the Galaxy*.
2   BBC (n.d.) BBC [Online]. Available at https://www.bbc.co.uk/programmes/b09rdv80.
3   McCrum, K. (2015) Daily Mirror [Online]. Available at http://www.mirror.co.uk/news/weird-news/rail-company-reveals-strangest-items-5969359.
4   1 Peter 2:11 (NLT).
5   See 1 Peter 2:8 (NIV).
6   See Colossians 1:15 (NIV).

7   bcponline (n.d.) bcponline.org [Online]. Available at https://www.bcponline.org/GreatLitany/Litany.html.

8   John 14:14 (NIV).

Session 5

1   Church of England (n.d.) Church of England [Online]. Available at https://www.churchofengland.org/prayer-and-worship/worship-texts-and-resources/book-common-prayer/public-baptism-infants.

2   Quotes.net (n.d.) Quotes.net [Online]. Available at https://www.quotes.net/quote/50309.

3   Evening Standard (2013) Evening Standard [Online]. Available at https://www.standard.co.uk/showbiz/celebrity-news/gary-barlow-elton-john-stucky-by-me-through-thick-and-thin-8969289.html.

Session 6

1   Ecology.com (n.d.) Ecology.com [Online]. Available at http://www.ecology.com/birth-death-rates/.

2   See Psalm 121 (NIV).

3   See Death is nothing at all by Henry Scott Holland.

4   Mangan, L. (2016) The Guardian [Online]. Available at https://www.theguardian.com/tv-and-radio/2016/apr/20/victoria-wood-her-shining-genius-never-stopped-unfurling.

5   Trustees for Methodist Church Purposes, 1999, Methodist Worship Book: Funeral Service leading to Committal, p. 457.

Appendix 2 – Further Reading/ Bibliography

Bond, G.M., *Jesus said "I am"*, Bible Society, 1987

Connelly, D., *The 'I am' sayings of Christ*, Scripture Union, 2007

Duff, J., 'The I am sayings', in *Guidelines*, May–Aug 2014, BRF, Abingdon, 2014

Grainger, R., 'The sacraments as rites of passage', in *Worship* 58 no. 3, 1984

Koester, C.R., *Symbolism in the Fourth Gospel*, Fortress Press, Minneapolis, 2003

Milne, B., *The Message of John*, IVP, Nottingham, 1993

Morrris, K. and Morris, R., *Leading Better Bible Studies*, Aquila Press, Sydney, 2008

Siler, M.M., 'Rites of Passage: a meeting of worship and pastoral care', in *Review and Expositor* 85, No. 1 Winter, 1988

CIRCLE
BOOKS

CHRISTIAN FAITH

Circle Books explores a wide range of disciplines within the field of Christian faith and practice. It also draws on personal testimony and new ways of finding and expressing God's presence in the world today.
If you have enjoyed this book, why not tell other readers by posting a review on your preferred book site.

Recent bestsellers from Circle Books are:

I Am With You (Paperback)
John Woolley

These words of divine encouragement were given to John Woolley
in his work as a hospital chaplain, and have since inspired and
uplifted tens of thousands, even changed their lives.
Paperback: 978-1-90381-699-8 ebook: 978-1-78099-485-7

God Calling
A. J. Russell

365 messages of encouragement channelled from Christ to two
anonymous "Listeners".
Hardcover: 978-1-905047-42-0 ebook: 978-1-78099-486-4

The Long Road to Heaven
A Lent Course Based on the Film
Tim Heaton

This second Lent resource from the author of *The Naturalist and the
Christ* explores Christian understandings of "salvation" in a five-
part study based on the film *The Way*.
Paperback: 978-1-78279-274-1 ebook: 978-1-78279-273-4

Abide In My Love
More Divine Help for Today's Needs
John Woolley

The companion to *I Am With You*, *Abide In My Love* offers words of
divine encouragement.
Paperback: 978-1-84694-276-1

From the Bottom of the Pond
The Forgotten Art of Experiencing God in the Depths of the
Present Moment
Simon Small
From the Bottom of the Pond takes us into the depths of the present
moment, to the only place where God can be found.
Paperback: 978-1-84694-066-8 ebook: 978-1-78099-207-5

God Is A Symbol Of Something True
Why You Don't Have to Choose Either a Literal Creator God or a
Blind, Indifferent Universe
Jack Call
In this examination of modern spiritual dilemmas, Call offers the
explanation that some of the most important elements of life are
beyond our control: everything is fundamentally alright.
Paperback: 978-1-84694-244-0

The Scarlet Cord
Conversations With God's Chosen Women
Lindsay Hardin Freeman, Karen N. Canton
Voiceless wax figures no longer, twelve biblical women,
outspoken, independent, faithful, selfless risk-takers, come to life
in *The Scarlet Cord*.
Paperback: 978-1-84694-375-1

Will You Join in Our Crusade?
The Invitation of the Gospels Unlocked by the Inspiration of Les
Miserables
Steve Mann
Les Miserables' narrative is entwined with Bible study in this book
of 42 daily readings from the Gospels, perfect for Lent or anytime.
Paperback: 978-1-78279-384-7 ebook: 978-1-78279-383-0

A Quiet Mind

Uniting Body, Mind and Emotions in Christian Spirituality
Eva McIntyre
A practical guide to finding peace in the present moment that will
change your life, heal your wounds and bring you a quiet mind.
Paperback: 978-1-84694-507-6 ebook: 978-1-78099-005-7

Readers of ebooks can buy or view any of these bestsellers by
clicking on the live link in the title. Most titles are published in
paperback and as an ebook. Paperbacks are available in traditional
bookshops. Both print and ebook formats are available online.

Find more titles and sign up to our readers' newsletter at
http://www.johnhuntpublishing.com/christianity. Follow us on
Facebook at https://www.facebook.com/ChristianAlternative.